TOW TRUCKS

WORKING TRUCKS

PAUL ZACHARY

EZ READERS

Creating Young Nonfiction Readers

EZ Readers lets children delve into nonfiction at beginning reading levels. Young readers are introduced to new concepts, facts, ideas, and vocabulary.

Tips for Reading Nonfiction with Beginning Readers

Talk about Nonfiction
Begin by explaining that nonfiction books give us information that is true. The book will be organized around a specific topic or idea, and we may learn new facts through reading.

Look at the Parts
Most nonfiction books have helpful features. Our *EZ Readers* include a Contents page, an index, a picture glossary, and color photographs. Share the purpose of these features with your reader.

Contents
Located at the front of a book, the Contents displays a list of the big ideas within the book and where to find them.

Index
An index is an alphabetical list of topics and the page numbers where they are found.

Picture Glossary
Located at the back of the book, a picture glossary contains key words/phrases that are related to the topic.

Photos/Charts
A lot of information can be found by "reading" the charts and photos found within nonfiction text. Help your reader learn more about the different ways information can be displayed.

With a little help and guidance about reading nonfiction, you can feel good about introducing a young reader to the world of *EZ Readers* nonfiction books.

Mitchell Lane
PUBLISHERS

2001 SW 31st Avenue
Hallandale, FL 33009
www.mitchelllane.com

First Edition, 2019.

Author: Paul Zachary
Designer: Ed Morgan
Editor: Sharon F. Doorasamy

Names/credits:
Title: Tow Trucks / by Paul Zachary
Description: Hallandale, FL : Mitchell Lane Publishers, [2019]

Series: Working Trucks

Library bound ISBN: 9781680203042

eBook ISBN: 9781680203059

EZ readers is an imprint of Mitchell Lane Publishers

Photo credits: Getty Images, Freepik.com

Library of Congress Cataloging-in-Publication Data
Names: Zachary, Paul, author.
Title: Tow trucks / by Paul Zachary.
Description: First edition. | Hallandale, FL : Mitchell Lane Publishers, [2019] | Series: Working trucks | Includes index.
Identifiers: LCCN 2018016801| ISBN 9781680203042 (library bound) | ISBN 9781680203059 (ebook)
Subjects: LCSH: Wreckers (Vehicles)—Juvenile literature.
Classification: LCC TL230.5.W74 Z33 2019 | DDC 629.225—dc23
LC record available at https://lccn.loc.gov/2018016801

CONTENTS

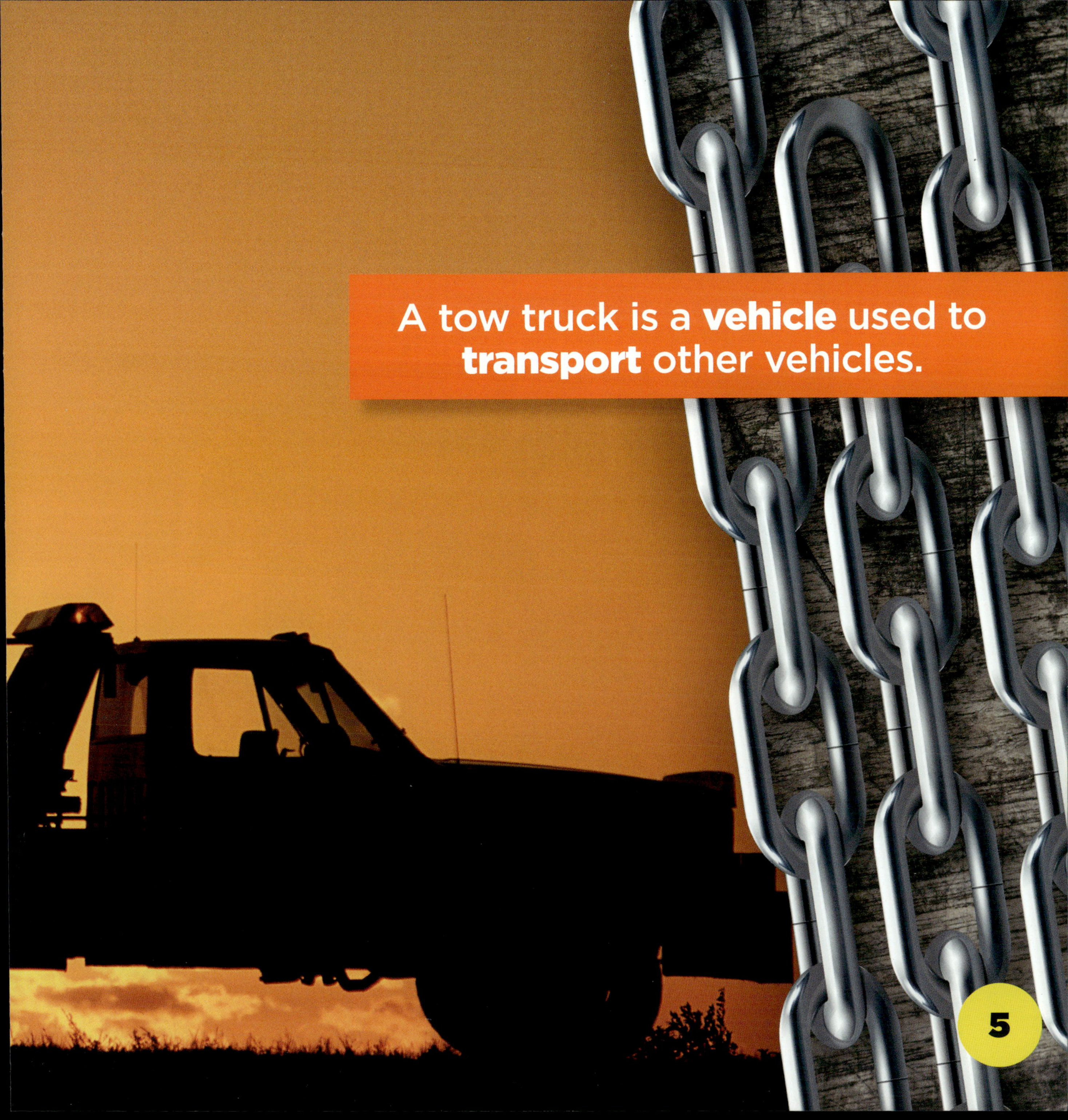

A tow truck is a **vehicle** used to **transport** other vehicles.

There are different kinds of tow trucks. **Flatbed** trucks carry their vehicles instead of pulling them.

Large carrier trucks transport many cars at one time.

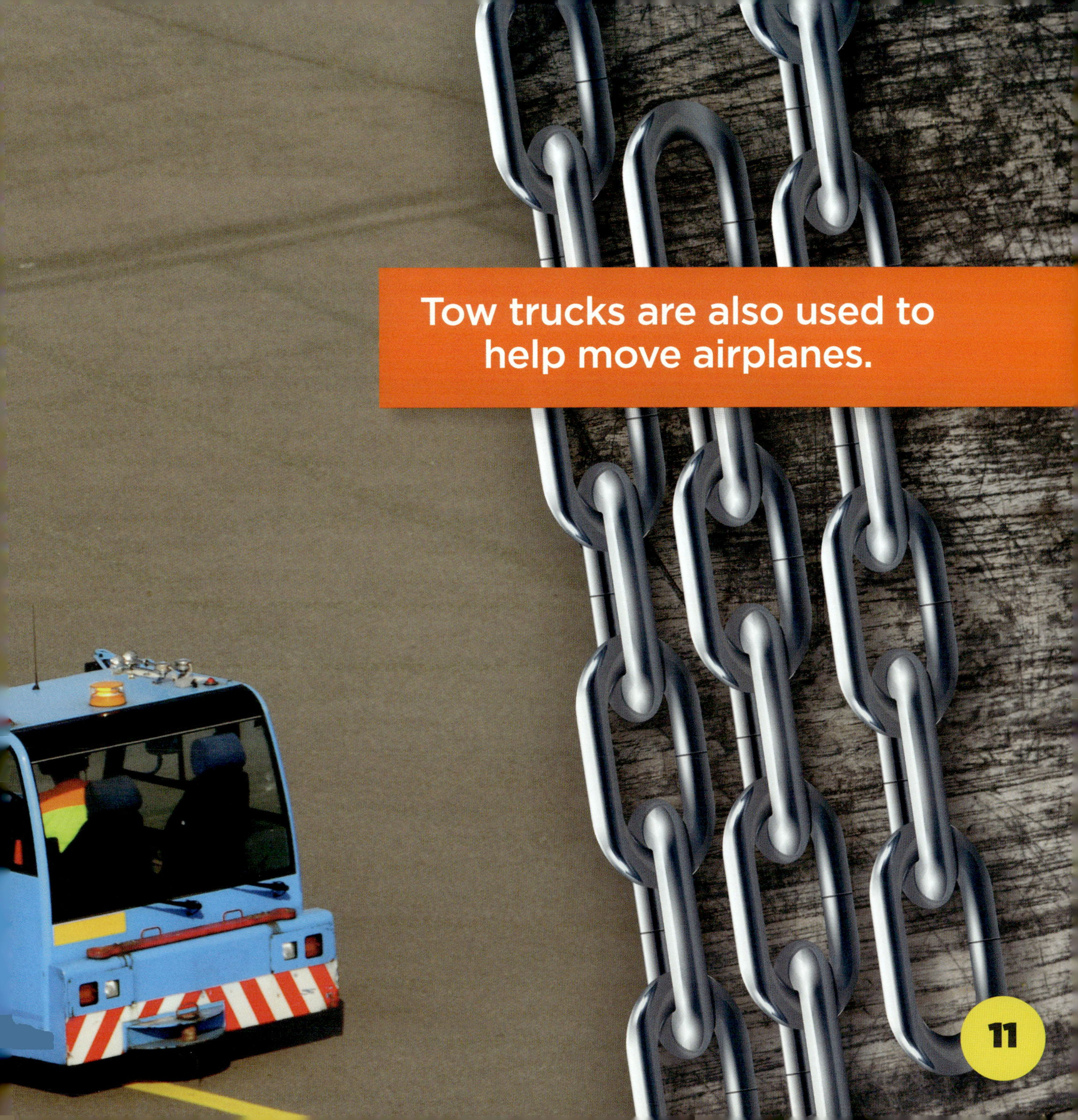

Tow trucks are also used to help move airplanes.

This car will be towed after an **accident** in a snow storm.

After an auto accident, tow trucks bring **damaged** cars to the local **auto repair shop**.

This **powerful** tow truck lifts a truck after a **rollover** accident.

17

The arm on this tow truck is called a boom. It is the boom that allows the truck to lift heavy vehicles.

Tow trucks have a towing cable that attaches to the vehicle that will be towed.

GLOSSARY

accident
An event that occurs by mistake

auto repair shop
A place of business that fixes damaged cars

damaged
Harm done to something

flatbed
A truck that has a level body with no sides or roof

powerful
Having a lot of strength or force

rollover
An accident in which a car turns over

transport
To move things from one place to another

vehicle
A machine that transports people or things

INTERESTING FACTS

The tow truck was invented in 1916 by Ernest Holmes Sr.

There is a museum dedicated to the tow truck. It is located in Chattanooga, Tennessee.

INDEX

24